Do You Listen?

by Joanne Mattern

Reading consultant: Susan Nations, M.Ed., author/
literacy coach/consultant in literacy development

WEEKLY READER®
PUBLISHING

Please visit our web site at: www.garethstevens.com
For a free color catalog describing our list of high-quality books,
call 1-800-542-2595 (USA) or 1-800-387-3178 (Canada).

Library of Congress Cataloging-in-Publication Data

Mattern, Joanne.
     Do you listen? / Joanne Mattern.
       p. cm. — (Are you a good friend?)
     Includes bibliographical references and index.
     ISBN-10: 0-8368-8274-1 (lib. bdg.)
     ISBN-13: 978-0-8368-8274-2 (lib. bdg.)
     ISBN-10: 0-8368-8279-2 (softcover)
     ISBN-13: 978-0-8368-8279-7 (softcover)
     1. Listening—Juvenile literature. 2. Friendship in children—
Juvenile literature. I. Title.
  BF323.L5M36   2008
  153.6'8—dc22   2007011022

First published in 2008 by
Weekly Reader® Books
An imprint of Gareth Stevens Publishing
1 Reader's Digest Road
Pleasantville, NY 10570-7000 USA

Copyright © 2008 by Gareth Stevens, Inc.

Editor: Gini Holland
Art direction: Tammy West
Graphic designer: Dave Kowalski
Picture research: Diane Laska-Swanke
Photographer: Gregg Andersen
Production: Jessica Yanke

Printed in the United States of America

1 2 3 4 5 6 7 8 9 11 10 09 08 07

Note to Educators and Parents

Reading is such an exciting adventure for young children! They are beginning to integrate their oral language skills with written language. To encourage children along the path to early literacy, books must be colorful, engaging, and interesting; they should invite the young reader to explore both the print and the pictures.

The *Are You a Good Friend?* series is designed to help children learn the special social skills they need to make and keep friends in their homes, schools, and communities. The books in this series teach the social skills of listening, sharing, helping others, and taking turns, showing readers how and why these skills help establish and maintain good friendships.

Each book is specially designed to support the young reader in the reading process. The familiar topics are appealing to young children and invite them to read — and reread — again and again. The full-color photographs and enhanced text further support the student during the reading process.

In addition to serving as wonderful picture books in schools, libraries, homes, and other places where children learn to love reading, these books are specifically intended to be read within an instructional guided reading group. This small group setting allows beginning readers to work with a fluent adult model as they make meaning from the text. After children develop fluency with the text and content, the books can be read independently. Children and adults alike will find these books supportive, engaging, and fun!

— Susan Nations, M.Ed., author, literacy coach,
and consultant in literacy development

Are you a good friend? One way to be a good friend is to **listen**. Do you know how to listen?

Listening is more than **hearing**. Listening also means thinking about what you are hearing. There are many ways to listen to a friend.

You can listen to a friend
read a story. Listening can
be fun.

9

You can listen to a friend tell a joke. Listening can be funny!

If a friend needs help, you can listen to him. Listening lets you know what to do.

Sometimes, a friend is sad. You can listen to him share his **feelings**.

Look at people when they talk. Looking shows you are listening.

Wait to speak until your friend is done talking. You cannot talk and listen at the same time!

Listening shows that you **care** about your friend. Listening helps you be a good friend.

Glossary

care — to like and want to help someone

feelings — emotions, including happiness, sadness, anger, hope, and fear

hearing — taking in sounds through the ears

listen — to think about what people are saying while they are talking

For More Information

How to Be a Friend. Laurie Krasny Brown (Little, Brown Young Readers)

Listen and Learn. Learning to Get Along (series). Cheri J. Meiners (Free Spirit Publishing)

We Can Listen. You and Me (series). Denise M. Jordan (Heinemann Library)

Why Should I Listen? Claire Llewellyn (Barron's Educational)

Index

About the Author

Joanne Mattern has written more than 150 books for children. Joanne also works in her local library. She lives in New York State with her husband, three daughters, and assorted pets. She enjoys animals, music, reading, going to baseball games, and visiting schools to talk about her books.